Advice to My Kids on Dating and Relationships...

Johanus Haidner

Published by Randwulf Publishing Inc., 2018, Canada

http://RandwulfPublishing.com
Printed by CreateSpace, an Amazon.com company.

ISBN: 0987887335
ISBN-13: 978-0-9878873-3-7

DEDICATION

Most of these are things I wish I had understood as a teenager and young adult. While my mom and I talked, we were never as open as I think we could have been. And certainly not as much as we are now. Nor as much as I am with my kids. I wrote this with my son and daughter in mind. And so it's addressed to them. But most of the advice is good for anyone, of any age.

So, this is dedicated to kids and teens everywhere, regardless of age. And to those who still need to learn, even though they're not kids anymore. And that could be all of us who want better relationships

ACKNOWLEDGMENTS

My kids are my inspiration in this. Without them, I wouldn't have had the idea at all. Also, thanks to Samson, who gave me the idea of publishing on kindle, and Jeff, who always believed.

Making the First Move

To my daughter on **Initiation...** If you find yourself without a date, but believe that it's a man's job to ask you out, then don't complain about not having a date.

And to my son and daughter about **assertiveness**....

We're in an age and society when people are considered equal. Don't be shy! Being shy won't get you further ahead in a lot of things in life, including dating. And don't be coy, either. Yes, they are two different things. If either of you finds someone interesting, you have to let that person know. People can be clueless. They can't read minds. How are you going to ever get ahead in a relationship - or even get the one you really want - if you don't let your feelings be known? Yes, it's hard. But not saying anything only leaves you without anything. Stand up for yourself, and approach that person you like, as long as it's in a respectful manner.

Fitting In

Everyone wants to fit in and be liked. But trying to change who you are in order to be liked by someone is dishonest. And it's hurtful -- to yourself, and to them. If you try to fit in to someone else's expectations you are only setting both yourself and them up for disappointment. That is why so often it's said that the best advice is to just be yourself.

On Looks

Yes, looks are important for a lot of things, including courting. Be clean, be tidy, take care of your body. But there is more than just looks. Being pretty/handsome and nice isn't enough. Be interesting, have opinions, know how to be social and hold a conversation. This goes far beyond dating. It will also help you in friendships, business, and your career (whatever that may be).

Sexuality

Whether you come home with a man, or a woman, they better make you happy. I don't care about your sexuality; I only care about your overall happiness. Sure I want grandkids. If it doesn't happen, c'est la vie. That's my problem, not yours. Find the person that you click with, and with whom you can be yourself, in love and friendship. And if it's more than one person, I'll deal with that, too. Just remember that if your sexuality is anything but heterosexual monogamy not everyone will accept it, and there will be extra struggles. But you'll have me by your side, always!

Race and Culture

Whether you come home with a white date, a black date, purple, green, or any colour there is, I don't care. And it shouldn't matter to anyone else. Yes, culture can present some issues. Be aware of those, and learn how to deal with the differences in a way that makes you both happy. Compromises will be necessary; realize that! And never put up with an ultimatum you can't handle for the rest of your life. Changing your religion to please your partner is never worth it. That is something you have to do for yourself and from deep, core beliefs. Stick to your beliefs; they are part of who you are.

Age

Make it legal and don't be weird.

If when you turn 18, that 30, 40, or 50 year old man (or woman) is suddenly interested in you, chances are you'll be in for a bad time. Being attracted to someone older is fine; as long as those older ones aren't looking for someone they can control, which is, unfortunately, often the case. If s/he's willing to meet me long before you two get intimate, then that is a positive sign. If s/he actually does, that is even better. Same with meeting your mother!

Dating Conversations

Almost no topic should be off the table when getting to know a date, whether it's the first date, or the twentieth. If that makes your date uncomfortable, find a new date. This simply means that you're not compatible. Better to find this out sooner than later.

There is a difference between talking about your desire to one day have children, and telling your date, "We'd make cute babies." on the first meeting. Don't be weird in your conversations. This can come across as really strange, creepy, or crazy. Learn the art of conversation and how to talk about things in a comfortable, easy manner. This will do you good in dating, as well as other aspects of your life.

Locale

The first date isn't about impressing the other person, it's about getting to know the other person. Where you go doesn't matter. Go bowling. Go to a movie. Throw axes! Drink some coffer or hot chocolate. Go skating. Just chill in the park. Don't expect the first date to be a romantic getaway of epic proportions. Low key, casual, and fun. If you want to be impressed, you're not ready for a relationship.

Paying and Money

Insist that you split the bill on the first date. For subsequent dates, follow the "the one who invites, pays" rule, or split the bill (in a manner you can both agree on).

If you can't afford to take yourself out on a date, then don't expect someone else to. This is where expectations can be an issue. Never expect someone to pay for you! And never put up with someone who expects you to pay for them. This is a bad precedent, as it leads to resentment and mistrust. Always be open with whomever you are dating about these expectations. If the person is worth being with, then s/he will understand and come to an agreement that can make you both happy.

Openness and Honesty

Say what you feel. Don't hint. Expect the same from your date. Openness is a necessity in good communication. And all good relationships require really good communication! It won't always be easy. And it won't always be kind. But it is necessary for any relationship to last.

Equality

To my daughter: No, your date doesn't have to open the door for you, because you're a woman. No, your date doesn't have to walk close to the street, because you're a woman. No, your date doesn't have to pay for you, because you're a woman. No, you aren't special, just because you are a woman. You are special because you are you, and that doesn't need to be validated via lousy or stupid gender expectations.

To my son: No, you don't have to hold open the door, pay for dinners, hold her coat, or any of the other gender specific behaviours that many consider "gentlemanly". This are antiquated ideas, and our society has grown past that. If your date requires these things, see what I wrote above. There are other ways that can validate her as a person, and she should appreciate you for who you are, not for you going out of your way to do things for her. If she places too many demands upon you, she is not your friend; she is only using you. Don't be her bitch.

Courtesy

Don't always expect your date to come to you. Offer to meet halfway. Maintain a balance on the first date. Courtesy shows that you care about your date. And expecting courtesy shows that you care about yourself. Make sure you maintain a balance, and over the relationship it becomes easy.

Being Used

Yes there are jerks in this world who will use people just for their looks, money, or for sex. Don't be one of them. And try to be aware of them. Sometimes it's hard, because they can be really slick and appear to be nice. If you feel, even for a minute, that you are being used, you probably are. If you need to ask someone for advice about it, talk to those you know really care about you - your friends, or even me (yes, I know that can be hard, because I'm your dad). People who really care about you will tell you what they really think, even if it's uncomfortable. And that can help you from being used by a jerk.

Choosing Your Date

Dating is about learning who someone is and isn't. It's essentially a trial for finding your partner. If you can't imagine living with the person and spending hours and hours on end with them, then they are not right for you. If you wouldn't want to spend your life with a person, don't date them. Breaking up can be hard, since hurting people (and being hurt) is never pleasant. But it's better a little pain now than a lot later. Choose carefully! There's nothing wrong with having standards and being a little picky. You want someone who matches you.

Safety and Drinking

Never leave your drink unattended. Either make sure you can always see it, or that it's left with someone you trust. That guy/gal you've been on a few dates with doesn't count.

People can be shits. While it's *extremely* rare for someone to spike a drink, odds less than are numerically worth mentioning, it can happen. And, yes, it happens to guys, too. Just be safe. More often it isn't about spiking the drink, it's about topping it up without your knowledge, thus getting you far more inebriated that you ever intended. And that's not safe either. Just don't trust your drink with anyone!

Safety and Location

Let a friend or family member know where you are, always. Whenever you go on a date or out with a new friend, it's good to let someone you know and trust where you are. Let them know of any significant changes (going to a different bar/restaurant or whatever). Let them know who the person is you're on a date with. Let them know when you've arrived safely home. This is so that everyone feels comfortable, and if anything happens, you have a safety net.

Safety and Rides

Whether you decide to sleep with your date or not, do not drive together until trust is solidified, however many dates it takes. Either take your own vehicle, or make liberal use of a taxi, especially when drinking is involved. Call me if you have to! I don't care how old you are. I'm always there to help.

Only when you have control over where you're going can you ensure your safety. Why take a chance, just because assault is rare? If someone else controls where you're driving to, you could end up somewhere you don't want to be. And if alcohol is involved, there is more risk than just that. Can you be certain the other person is completely sober? Or, with legal drugs in our society, not high? Not being straight is the biggest risk of all! Don't take that risk.

Safety and Space

Do not invite anyone to your home right away! The number of times people invite another to their homes, without having physically met the other person previously, is baffling. Don't do that. Ever! It takes a while to get to know another person. There is no way, ever, that you could know another person well enough after meeting them for only a few hours to be 100% certain that person is safe to be with, especially intimately. And that starts the next point...

Sex

It's okay if you don't want to have sex, and the reason doesn't matter. It's also okay if your partner doesn't want to have sex, and the reason doesn't matter. Never pressure your partner into sex. Be nice about it, always! And never let yourself be pressured into sex. That is manipulative, and can be abusive. Again, abuse should never be tolerated. It's also okay if you want to have sex. Just be safe about it.

Consent

In a perfect world, consent will always be asked for and explicitly known. This isn't a perfect world. Make your voice loud, and your consent clear. Also make sure your partner's consent is clear and certain. Don't be afraid to say "No!" If that doesn't work, do everything in your power to get away. Threat of police action is certainly acceptable and on the table. Get away! If it's an issue, use any means you have to. And then call me! And, if the situation warrants it, call the police.

Diseases

Having the STD talk can be awkward, but it's also a good metric to use when determining compatibility. If your prospective date balks at the idea of discussing testing frequency and safe methods of sex, then run for the hills. This is not a person you want to trust, nor is it someone who is comfortable communicating with important matters. If something as straightforward and simple as this is an issue for that person, then how tough will it be to communicate when there are other issues on the table? Especially when strong emotions and life decisions are to be made?

Condoms

Condoms don't protect against every STD, and they aren't 100% effective against pregnancy, either -- nothing is, except abstinence. Better a 98% chance than a 0% chance. *"I just can't feel anything with condoms"*, is almost always an excuse, at least 99% of the time. Even if it's not, it doesn't trump your safety. Remember, safety first!

Entitlement

Entitlement is bad, and it is the catalyst for many of the issues in dating. That said, entitlement comes from gender expectations. You're not to blame for entitlement, but neither should you perpetuate it by expecting your partner to fulfill certain "roles". No woman is entitled to have her date pay for her, just as no man is entitled to sex (and vice-versa). While there are some places for gender roles, in our day and age these are much more flexible, and roles within couples must be determined by the two people involved. And neither one is automatically entitled to anything within those role structures!

Manipulation

If your goal in dating is to get free meals/free drinks/free anything, and not to seek a relationship, be upfront about that expectation. Expect the same from your date. Don't be manipulative and cagey. This behaviour is bad for both people involved. And don't put up with it, either!

More on Manipulation

Sex is not a weapon to be wielded, or a hostage negotiation tool. For either of you. Any relationship that uses affection, whether it be hugs and kisses or sex, as a way to manipulate another person is an unhealthy relationship. And the person doing that manipulating is being abusive. Abuse of any sort is not to be tolerated. Period. End of game.

Insecurity

Talking about past partners and relationships isn't a bad thing. Don't allow the fact that people have had a life before you make you feel jealous. And don't let the other person guilt you in any way about it. If they are that insecure, chances are they will also be abusive at some point. Deal with it right away! And if it continues, get away. Jealousy and insecurity will eventually destroy any relationship.

Contingency Plans

Never allow yourself to rely completely on your partner. If the relationship doesn't work out, never allow yourself to be in a position where you can't survive on your own. It doesn't matter if the relationship is 3 weeks old, or 17 months old, or 15 years old. You still need to have your independence and be able to fend for yourself. Always have a backup plan. And always know that you can come to me with anything! I will help you out, no matter what, to the best of my abilities.

Deal Breakers

It's okay to have them. It's okay to change your mind. It's okay to be stubborn about your deal breakers. They're yours. It doesn't matter what your deal breaker is. If someone makes fun of you or belittles you for your preferences and deal breakers, that person isn't worth being around anyhow. If it's your date's friend, or your friend, then that friend is toxic. What does it say about your date for choosing that other person to hang out with? And what does that say about your "friend" for making fun of you?

Walls

Don't let them build. We all know that walls are psychological barriers. They hold yourself in and protect you. But they also keep everyone out, including those who love you and can help to protect you. The longer you stay in unhealthy relationships, the taller your walls will grow. The taller your wall grows, the easier it is for you to keep adding to them, making those walls stronger. If you find yourself building walls, it's a sign that the relationship is toxic. It's time to end it. Knock that crap down!

Privacy

You, and your date or partner, are still allowed privacy. Don't expect passwords to phones, emails, social media, etc. And don't put up with demands for these, either. Again, this is manipulative and displays a serious lack of trust and a lot of insecurity. Every person needs and deserves some privacy.

A Harsh Reality

If all of your dates/partners are "crazy", the common denominator is you. Let's find you a good counsellor or therapist. There is no shame in going to therapy or counselling, and this can help you deal with whatever issues there are that are preventing you from having healthy relationships. If you can't afford it, there are plenty of places that offer it for really cheap or free. Or I can pay. Let's just get your issues dealt with so that you can move forward and live a healthy, happy life, and have great relationships!

Trust

If you don't trust your partner, or if he/she doesn't trust you, then it's done. The why doesn't matter. It's as simple as that. Trust can, and should, be earned; but some people will never be worthy of it. And some people are never capable of giving it. Neither of these are healthy. Make this a deal breaker!

Power

The moment your date, or partner, attempts to create a balance of power, leave. Power, and the wrestling to achieve it, does not belong in a healthy relationship. Only strive for healthy relationships!

Abuse

This is an extension of power. Abuse, whether physical or mental/emotional is never acceptable. This moment such a thing happens, leave. It's never worth the effort to be with someone who plays these games or does this kind of damage to another, whether physical or psychological. Just get out! It doesn't matter if you have to leave everything you own behind. Those are only things, and they can be replaced. Your family will always help you. Your well being is more important than anything money can buy. Just get out and go wherever you can, even if it's a shelter or a friend's couch. And you're always welcome at my home... Always. Abuse if never acceptable!

Sexual Abuse

Such abuse is never, and will never, be your fault. I will always be there to tell you this, and help you through it, in the event of it happening. And as soon as you're able, the authorities should be informed. This will not only help you to get over it, but it could protect another person in the future.

Other People's Opinions

Yes, you'll get these. Too often your friends will be all approving of a person you date, thinking they're awesome... Until you break up, then they'll say things disparaging that person --

"S/he was never good enough for you..."

"I always thought X was a jerk, anyways..."

"I never liked X..."

If those things were true, they should have told you that *before* you broke up. Let your friends know that! And why they should be upfront and honest with you. The same goes for your family.

If I don't like someone you're dating, there's a reason. I have more experience with people. I have an outside perspective and can see things you may not be able to. I want you to be happy, enjoy life and a partner, have kids and a relationship that is amazing and wonderful! If I don't like your date, then I think that person isn't able to give you those things, as you deserve them. If you disagree, then we should talk about it. Better that you and I understand each other's perspectives and learn why one of us could be wrong than to hold onto the feelings and fear for the other or about what the other thinks or feels. Same goes for your friends.

Don't Chase Carrots

No matter what bright thing is there, being held in front of you, if it's there to entice you into a relationship or doing something you're uncomfortable with, chances are it's not worth it in the long run. Carrot chasing is a way of letting yourself be manipulated. Don't do it! Remember that no healthy relationship is ever built upon manipulation.

Believe in Yourself

Don't let anyone discourage you or put you
down, especially in a relationship. You will
always have worth, you just may not know what
it is at the time. And always approach things
with confidence and trust in yourself.
Confidence is extremely attractive, whether to a
man or a woman. And it helps in many other
aspects of life, not just relationships. Whatever
you set out to do, don't let anyone cut you
down, even me or your mom. And especially
not someone who is a potential partner! Partners
support and believe in each other, without taking
advantage of that belief. And failure is only a
learning step towards something better. Even if
a relationship fails, you need to believe in
yourself, as a failed relationship teaches you what
is better for you and how to be a better partner
in your next relationship.

Don't Make Your Partner Your First Priority

It doesn't matter who they are or how much you love them (or think you love them), you always have to put yourself first. You are no good to anyone, even your partner, if you don't take care of yourself. And for most people, you are just an option. There is always someone else you can find to love you. Always!

Communication

Honesty is to communication what multiplication is to calculus. If you can't be honest, you can't communicate. Honesty is the minimum, not the maximum; there is more to communication than just honesty.

—Jenna Medaris

Communication is the most important aspect of any healthy relationship. But it's not always easy... Learning to communicate means making yourself vulnerable and accepting your partner's vulnerability. Be prepared! And don't let emotions get in the way. That is the surest way to shut communication down. It will be tough at times. So learn! Always try to learn more about communicating with your partner, and learn about your partner and yourself.

Expectations and Goals

These are two things that make or break all relationships. Every couple I've ever spoken with whose relationship has lasted more than 30 years agrees that mutual goals and expectations within the relationship are what keeps them together. Yes, love, understanding, communication, and respect are all necessary. But it is the desire to move in the same direction through life that is most sustaining, and helps to foster all of the other necessary components in a relationship. Be clear about your expectations and goals, in life and in the relationship. And be certain that your partner is, too.

Sacrifices

These are similar to compromises, and they will happen. Anyone that tells you differently is probably a manipulator that always gets their way. Don't be the one who always sacrifices. And don't be the manipulator! A good relationship has both give and take in it. And don't keep count. Relationships aren't about keeping score.

Marriage

Get married, or don't, I don't care, as long as whatever you decide to do is shared by your partner. Again, communicate about this, and if what you want isn't compatible with your partner's desires, then maybe you really shouldn't be together. There are always other people out there. Never waste time with someone you're uncertain of in the long term.

In-Laws

When (if) you marry someone, you do not marry their family, despite what you've heard. Just because those people are now legally members of the family, that doesn't mean you need to invite them to your home, or suffer their company, if you don't like them. If they are crappy people, then don't put up with them! Yes, this might cause some strife with your spouse. Explain your feelings, and the reasons behind them. If your spouse really loves you, then there will be a way that you can both deal with it on an equitable basis.

Support Networks

Everyone needs some kind of emotional support network outside of the relationship, whether family or friends (hopefully both). No relationship is successful without this! Maintaining such a network is one of the best things you can do to stay healthy. Also, other people offer an outside perspective on your relationship. That outside view can help cut through overwhelming emotion and help you see when (if) you're being treated badly, or if you're behaving poorly. This is invaluable!

Deep friendships also provide a space to talk through methods and plans for resolving conflict inside your romantic relationship. They also provide an outlet for all kinds of emotional stress, giving you the resilience to treat your partner better. Friendships where you can be yourself and be honest are a crucial tool for making any relationship work, and for combating unhealthy co-dependence.

Abusers try to cut their partners off from support networks. If this is happening to you, then this could be the first signs of an abusive relationship. That means it's time to draw on that support network and communicate with them, too. If your parents and/or friends have an issue with someone you are dating, it's time to pay closer attention to what's going on. These are people who care about you and what's best for you; they might see something or know something that you are refusing to see or don't know. Listen up!

A Final Word...

Yes, I know this might embarrass you, especially if your friends see it while you're still a teenager. That is minor in the grand scheme of things. I raised you, and tried my best to teach you how to be a kind, decent, responsible, conscientious person. All of the things I write here are things that I know I probably didn't need to tell you. You likely know them all already, as we've no doubt discussed them in one way or another. But I'm your father, and I worry. I worry, not because I don't believe you're capable of being good or taking care of yourself, but because you are my kid, and I will always worry. I want the best for you, and I want to spare you as much pain as I can. With that said, I'm sure that you will have the confidence you need to succeed in your life and your relationships. You're going to do just fine. I love you. Don't forget to call me!

Johanus Haidner lives and works in Edmonton, Alberta. Born and raised in Calgary, he has lived in Canada for most of his life. He finished up his MBA while living in Germany and spent a short while traveling around western Europe and has also visited Central Asia and a few other countries. He lived in Houston, Texas for two years after completing his university studies. He has been a military police officer, a teacher (grades 4 through 12), a cook, a baker, dealt several games in casinos, made concrete countertops, built a couple of high end, custom houses while managing a small construction company, worked as a graphic designer and editor, been a technical writer, worked as an internal auditor, a financial analyst, and spent more than fifteen years as an accountant. He now does small business taxes as his primary income, although his first loves have always been art and writing. He is a single dad of a boy and a girl, who are the most important parts of his life.

Mr. Haidner runs The Academy of European Swordsmanship (swordsmanship.ca) in his spare time teaching German (KdF) and English martial arts to people from all walks of life. aged seven and up. HEMA is fun!

*His kids inspire him every day. They are the most enthusiastic fans of his artwork as well as the **Mythic Hero** tabletop RPG game he wrote. He is working on many supplements to **Mythic Hero**, as well as writing some children's stories, a couple of novels, and some other non-fiction. Johanus also he sells his artwork, and his handcrafted jewellery and knives.*

Find more of his writing at johanushaidner.com.

You can find more of Johanus Haidner's work on his website (johanushaidner.com) or on Amazon.com or Amazon.ca.

Also search for Randwulf Publishing (or Mythic Hero) on Patreon for the **Mythic Hero** RPG. All Patrons receive the basic ruleset. Perks get better with each step up. Get maps, dungeons, adventure seeds, full modules, monsters, spells, special weapons, and more!